The Elephant with Small Ears

Written
and
Illustrated by

Cindy R. Lee

Cindy R. Lee, LCSW, LADC
PO Box 14060
Oklahoma City, OK 73113

The "listening and minding" concept was derived from the Trust-Based Relational Intervention ® resources (Purvis & Cross, 1999-2016.) For more information, please read Purvis, K.B., Cross, D.R. & Sunshine, W.L. (2007) *The Connected Child: Bringing Hope and Healing to Your Adoptive Family*. New York: McGraw-Hill.

Acknowledgements:
Thank you to Christopher, Amanda and Jack for all your advice, understanding and support. Thank you to Mutte, GiGi, Buzzy, Christie, Eric, Zachary and Emily for being a part of it all. Special thanks to Kelly and Amy Gray, David and Jean McLaughlin and the McLaughlin Family Foundation for giving the gift of healing to foster and adopted children. Thank you to Casey Call, Henry Milton and Jennifer Abney for all their support and guidance. Gratitude also goes to Cheryl Devoe for donating her time and editing skills to this project. Thank you to Sarah Mercado for all the support all of the time.

Thank you to all of you who have opened up your hearts to children from hard places and thank you to all of you who support families in their foster or adoptive journey. Words cannot express how grateful I am to Dr. Karyn Purvis and Dr. David Cross for creating an intervention that heals.

Dedicated to the beautiful children who inspired this story:

Brooklyn, Jaley, Winston, Jolee, & Gianna

In Memory of Dr. Karyn Purvis

Listening and Minding
Teaching Tips for Parents by Cindy R. Lee, LCSW, LADC

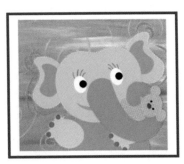

"My child does not follow directions" is one of the most common frustrations parents express. Parents ask their child to do something (or to stop doing something), and they get no response or an incorrect response. They ask again, this time with a stern voice, and still no action. Yelling or threats ensue, and the startled child finally begins to move.

Parents wonder, "Is my child ignoring me on purpose?" This is one option, but very rarely the case. Often they are not ignoring on purpose; they are simply enjoying whatever activity they are engaged in. Parents also explore the idea that something is physically wrong with the child's ability to hear. It is quite possible, but this second option is also rare. If you suspect this as a possibility, make a doctor's appointment and have your child's hearing checked!

So why do children not listen and mind? Let us consider a few options. Perhaps children were not taught HOW to listen and mind correctly? Or perhaps, due to their past experiences, their little minds are busy focusing on survival rather than following a caregiver's instructions. If the child in your care came from a hard place, they may feel the need to stay in control to stay safe. If the entire world around you was out of control, your survival reaction would also be to control any aspect of your life you could. If this describes your child, the need to control will only dissipate when the child feels safe and can trust. In order for the child to feel safe, caregivers need to avoid threats, yelling and punishment.

Although challenging behavior requires a correction for learning, punishment may not be the most effective avenue for changing behavior long term. In order for your child to learn the correct response, they have to practice the correct response. If you send your child to time-out because they failed to follow directions, they are never given the chance to follow through and learn HOW to follow directions. If you raise your voice to gain compliance, then it is possible your child has learned you really don't mean business until you start yelling. In addition, if you count to three, your child is likely to just wait until you get to three to act. Remember, children do not feel safe when they are being yelled at or threatened.

How do we teach our children to listen and mind and feel safe at the same time? Start by setting the child up for success and then practice "listening and minding" while playing fun games.

Set Your Child Up for Success

Embracing these tips will help you facilitate your child's success.

Gain Loving Eye Contact when Giving Instructions.
Of all the suggestions given in this handout, gaining eye contact is the most important one. Again, this is the most important change you can make as a parent. If your child is watching a favorite TV show and you shout from the kitchen "It's time for dinner," don't expect the child to hop right up. If you want success, walk over to them, gain eye contact and communicate your need (with a smile). If they have a history of not listening and minding, you can remain close until they start to move. This may seem like more work for you as a caregiver, but it is less frustrating and takes less energy than asking over and over again as your voice and anger escalate.

The "listening and minding" concept was derived from the Trust-Based Relational Intervention® resources (Purvis & Cross, 1999-2016.) Purvis, K.B., Cross, D.R. & Sunshine, W.L. (2007) *The Connected Child: Bringing Hope and Healing to Your Adoptive Family.* New York: McGraw-Hill.

Listening and Minding
Teaching Tips for Parents by Cindy R. Lee, LCSW, LADC

Offer Choices. Sharing power with your child is powerful. Offering choices increases the likelihood that your child will participate because the child feels safe and valued. For example, you can say, "It is time to do your homework. Would you like to start it now or in 5 minutes?" Or, "We need to have a vegetable with lunch. Would you like to eat carrots or a salad?"

Teach the Art of Compromise. Once you teach your child how to compromise, they feel empowered to communicate their needs to you. For example, you offer choices such as "It is time to do your homework. Would you like to start it now or in 5 minutes?" However, the child may have another choice in mind that is acceptable. They can then ask, "May I please have a compromise? May I please finish this show and then start my homework?" Teaching a child to verbalize their needs and follow instructions is priceless. Compromising and negotiating our needs are important communication skills for adults and children.

Model Respectful Communication. It is important to say please when we ask our children to do something. We are trying to teach them how to be respectful and they learn this from watching and listening to us. For example, rather than saying "Go brush your teeth," we need to model with "Please go brush your teeth."

Speak Affectionately with Detail and Praise. Asking your child to do something in a vague manner can be confusing. For example, if you ask your child to eat his veggies, he may take a bite or two without knowing that you are asking him to eat all of the veggies. If you ask your child to eat five bites of peas, he will eat five bites of peas. In addition, offering praise makes things more fun and feels safer. For example, you can say, "Please go brush your teeth and when you come back I will give you a high five." When they come back, give them a high five and tell them, "I am so proud of you for listening and minding!"

Instruction Should be Age Appropriate. Asking a child to do something they are not capable of produces frustration for the child and the caregiver. Knowing your child's capabilities can sometimes be difficult. Please remember that children with a history of trauma may be less than half their chronological age, both developmentally and emotionally. For example, a 10 year old child may have the emotional development of a five year old. This is complicated when they look and act their age in some ways, but not others. A qualified professional can assist you in understanding your child's capabilities. Keep in mind, all children are created with different capabilities and develop at different speeds.

Practice Listening and Minding

Play is the most effective way to teach a child a new skill. Try this fun game:

Gadget Get and Give

Gather 5 small gadgets or objects. While your child is watching, set them in various places around the room. Have your child stand in front of you and gain eye contact. Ask your child with respect to get the first item and bring it back to you. Have them respond with "ok daddy" or "ok mommy" after you give them the instruction. Each time they bring it back, give them a high five and say "good job listening and minding." You can even give the child a turn at giving commands. If you are both having fun, they are learning!

For more information, please read *The Connected Child* by Purvis, Cross and Lyons Sunshine or contact a professional that is familiar with the work of Dr. Purvis and Dr. Cross. A list of these professionals is available at www.child.tcu.edu.

The "listening and minding" concept was derived from the Trust-Based Relational Intervention® resources (Purvis & Cross, 1999-2016.) Purvis, K.B., Cross, D.R. & Sunshine, W.L. (2007) *The Connected Child: Bringing Hope and Healing to Your Adoptive Family.* New York: McGraw-Hill.

This is Elly the elephant.

She is very sad and scared.

Elly is scared because she lives with a new
mommy and daddy she does not know yet.

Because Elly is so scared, her ears will not grow.

An elephant with small ears
gets into lots of trouble.

With small ears, Elly is not able to
"listen and mind"
her mommy and daddy.

When Elly's new mommy asked Elly to brush her teeth,
her small ears did not hear mommy's words.

Mommy thought Elly was being disobedient,
so she sent Elly to time-out!

When daddy asked Elly to eat her dinner,
her small ears did not hear his words.

Elly's daddy sent her away and took her favorite toy.

He thought she was not "listening and minding."

When mommy asked Elly to sit in her chair,

Elly's small ears did not hear the words.

Elly's mommy yelled at Elly.

She thought Elly was not "listening and minding."

Then one day, a wise elephant
told Elly's new mommy and daddy,
"Elly's ears are small because
she is scared. Please do
not punish her for
having small ears."

The next day, Elly's mommy asked her to brush her teeth.
Understanding Elly was scared,
     her mommy looked into her eyes,
          gave her a hug,
               and helped her brush her teeth.

In that moment,

Elly was not scared,

and her mommy praised her for

"listening and minding."

Because Elly was not so scared,

her ears began to

grow.

Elly's daddy asked Elly to finish her dinner.

Elly still did not hear his words.

Instead of sending Elly to her room and

taking away her favorite toy,

he gazed into her eyes,

gave her a hug,

and kindly asked her to finish her dinner.

In that moment,

Elly was not scared

and she was able to eat her meal.

After she ate, her daddy told her,

"Good job listening and minding."

Because Elly

was less scared,

her ears

grew

even more.

Elly's mommy asked Elly to sit in her chair.
Elly still did not hear her words.

Instead of yelling at Elly, her mommy gave her a big hug, looked into her eyes and asked how she could help Elly sit in her chair.

In that moment,

Elly was able to accept help sitting in her chair.

Her loving parents told her,

"Good job listening

and minding."

Because Elly was

no longer scared

her ears grew

even bigger.

Elly's ears **grew so big!**

She was able to hear her mommy and daddy's words all the time.

Her mommy and daddy praised her often

for "listening and minding," and

Elly felt happy and safe

in her new home.

About the Author:

Cindy R. Lee is a Licensed Clinical Social Worker and Licensed Drug and Alcohol Counselor in private practice. Cindy is the co-founder and Executive Director of HALO Project, which is an intensive outpatient program for foster and adoptive children and their families. For more information please visit www.haloprojectokc.org. Cindy resides in Edmond, Oklahoma with her husband, children and pets.

The Elephant with Small Ears is one of eight children's books designed to teach Trust-Based Relational Intervention® (TBRI®) principles. TBRI® was developed by Dr. Karyn Purvis and Dr. David Cross from TCU's Institute of Child Development. For more information, please visit www.child.tcu.edu.

Other Titles:

It's Tough to be Gentle: A Dragon's Tale teaches "Gentle and Kind"

Baby Owl Lost Her Whoo teaches "Who's the Boss"

Doggie Doesn't Know No teaches "Accepting No"

The Penguin and the Fine-Looking Fish teaches "With Respect"

The Redo Roo teaches "The Redo"

Made in the USA
Monee, IL
01 February 2024

52686701R00021